Flamingos

Julie Murray

Abdo Kids Junior
is an Imprint of Abdo Kids
abdobooks.com

Abdo
INTERESTING ANIMALS
Kids

abdobooks.com

Published by Abdo Kids, a division of ABDO, P.O. Box 398166, Minneapolis, Minnesota 55439.

Printed in the United States of America, North Mankato, Minnesota.

102022

012023

THIS BOOK CONTAINS RECYCLED MATERIALS

Photo Credits: Getty Images, Shutterstock

Production Contributors: Teddy Borth, Jennie Forsberg, Grace Hansen

Design Contributors: Candice Keimig, Pakou Moua

Library of Congress Control Number: 2022937165

Publisher's Cataloging-in-Publication Data

Names: Murray, Julie, author.

Title: Flamingos / by Julie Murray

Description: Minneapolis, Minnesota : Abdo Kids, 2023 | Series: Interesting animals | Includes online resources and index.

Identifiers: ISBN 9781098264147 (lib. bdg.) | ISBN 9781098264703 (ebook) | ISBN 9781098264987 (Read-to-Me ebook)

Subjects: LCSH: Flamingos--Juvenile literature. | Birds--Behavior--Juvenile literature. | Animals--Juvenile literature. | Zoology--Juvenile literature.

Classification: DDC 598.3--dc23

Table of Contents

Flamingos

Flamingos are large birds.

They live around the world.

They like **shallow** lakes and swamps.

They have long legs and necks. Some stand more than 4 feet (1.2 m) tall.

They have big wings.

Their **wingspan** can be 5 feet (1.5 m).

They have a long bill. The bill helps them eat.

They eat seeds and **algae**.

They also eat **brine shrimp**.

Their feathers are pink.

The color comes from the food they eat.

Flamingos can stand and sleep on one leg.

They live in large groups called colonies.

Flamingo Features

big wings

long curved bill

long legs and neck

pink feathers

Glossary

algae
living things that mainly live in water and make their food like plants do.

brine shrimp
any of various small crustaceans that live in salty water.

shallow
not deep.

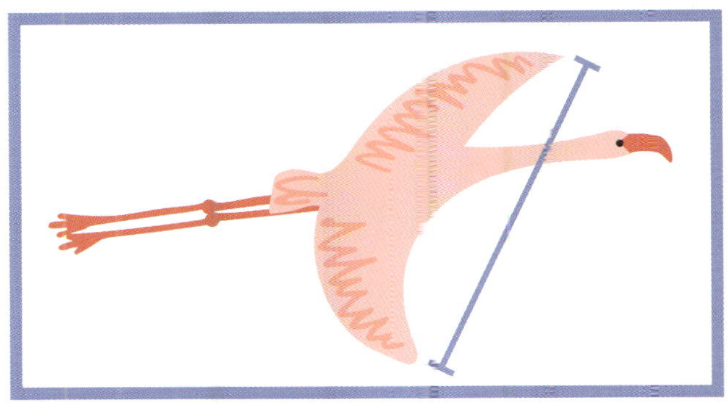

wingspan
the distance from the tip of one wing of a bird to the tip of the other.

Index